Savvy Saver's Expense Journal

Monthly Bill Notebook

@ Journals and Notebooks

Bill Log

________________ Month

✓	Date Paid	Bill Name	Amount	Due Date	Confirmation

Bill Log ________________ Month

Bill Log

______________ Month

✓	Date Paid	Bill Name	Amount	Due Date	Confirmation

Bill Log

_______________ Month

✓	Date Paid	Bill Name	Amount	Due Date	Confirmation

Bill Log

_______________ Month

✓	Date Paid	Bill Name	Amount	Due Date	Confirmation

Bill Log

_________________ Month

✓	Date Paid	Bill Name	Amount	Due Date	Confirmation

Bill Log

________________ Month

✓	Date Paid	Bill Name	Amount	Due Date	Confirmation

Bill Log

_______________ Month

✓	Date Paid	Bill Name	Amount	Due Date	Confirmation

Bill Log

_______________ Month

✓	Date Paid	Bill Name	Amount	Due Date	Confirmation

Bill Log

_________________ Month

✓	Date Paid	Bill Name	Amount	Due Date	Confirmation

Bill Log

_________________ Month

✓	Date Paid	Bill Name	Amount	Due Date	Confirmation

Bill Log

________________ Month

✓	Date Paid	Bill Name	Amount	Due Date	Confirmation

Bill Log

_______________ Month

	Date Paid	Bill Name	Amount	Due Date	Confirmation

Bill Log

_______________ Month

✓	Date Paid	Bill Name	Amount	Due Date	Confirmation

Bill Log

________________ Month

✓	Date Paid	Bill Name	Amount	Due Date	Confirmation

Bill Log

_________________ Month

✓	Date Paid	Bill Name	Amount	Due Date	Confirmation

Bill Log

__________________ Month

✓	Date Paid	Bill Name	Amount	Due Date	Confirmation

Bill Log

_______________ Month

✓	Date Paid	Bill Name	Amount	Due Date	Confirmation

Bill Log

_______________ Month

✓	Date Paid	Bill Name	Amount	Due Date	Confirmation

Bill Log

_______________ Month

✓	Date Paid	Bill Name	Amount	Due Date	Confirmation

Bill Log

_______________ Month

✓	Date Paid	Bill Name	Amount	Due Date	Confirmation

Bill Log

_________________ Month

✓	Date Paid	Bill Name	Amount	Due Date	Confirmation

Bill Log

_________________ Month

✓	Date Paid	Bill Name	Amount	Due Date	Confirmation

Bill Log

_______________ Month

✓	Date Paid	Bill Name	Amount	Due Date	Confirmation

Bill Log

_______________ Month

✓	Date Paid	Bill Name	Amount	Due Date	Confirmation

Bill Log

______________ Month

✓	Date Paid	Bill Name	Amount	Due Date	Confirmation

Bill Log

_______________ Month

✓	Date Paid	Bill Name	Amount	Due Date	Confirmation

Bill Log

_________________ Month

✓	Date Paid	Bill Name	Amount	Due Date	Confirmation

Bill Log

_______________ Month

✓	Date Paid	Bill Name	Amount	Due Date	Confirmation

Bill Log

_______________ Month

✓	Date Paid	Bill Name	Amount	Due Date	Confirmation
✓	Date Paid	Bill Name	Amount	Due Date	Confirmation

Bill Log

_______________ Month

✓	Date Paid	Bill Name	Amount	Due Date	Confirmation

Bill Log

_________________ Month

✓	Date Paid	Bill Name	Amount	Due Date	Confirmation

Bill Log

_______________ Month

✓	Date Paid	Bill Name	Amount	Due Date	Confirmation

Bill Log

_________________ Month

✓	Date Paid	Bill Name	Amount	Due Date	Confirmation

Bill Log

_________________ Month

✓	Date Paid	Bill Name	Amount	Due Date	Confirmation

Bill Log

_______________ Month

✓	Date Paid	Bill Name	Amount	Due Date	Confirmation

Bill Log

_______________ Month

✓	Date Paid	Bill Name	Amount	Due Date	Confirmation

Bill Log

_______________ Month

✓	Date Paid	Bill Name	Amount	Due Date	Confirmation

Bill Log

_______________ Month

✓	Date Paid	Bill Name	Amount	Due Date	Confirmation

Bill Log

_____________ Month

✓	Date Paid	Bill Name	Amount	Due Date	Confirmation

Bill Log

_______________ Month

✓	Date Paid	Bill Name	Amount	Due Date	Confirmation

Bill Log

_______________ Month

✓	Date Paid	Bill Name	Amount	Due Date	Confirmation

Bill Log

_______________ Month

✓	Date Paid	Bill Name	Amount	Due Date	Confirmation

Bill Log

____________ Month

✓	Date Paid	Bill Name	Amount	Due Date	Confirmation

Bill Log

_______________ Month

✓	Date Paid	Bill Name	Amount	Due Date	Confirmation

Bill Log

________________ Month

✓	Date Paid	Bill Name	Amount	Due Date	Confirmation

Bill Log

_________________ Month

✓	Date Paid	Bill Name	Amount	Due Date	Confirmation

Bill Log

____________ Month

✓	Date Paid	Bill Name	Amount	Due Date	Confirmation

Bill Log

_______________ Month

✓	Date Paid	Bill Name	Amount	Due Date	Confirmation

Bill Log

_________________ Month

✓	Date Paid	Bill Name	Amount	Due Date	Confirmation

Bill Log

_______________ Month

✓	Date Paid	Bill Name	Amount	Due Date	Confirmation

Bill Log

_______________ Month

✓	Date Paid	Bill Name	Amount	Due Date	Confirmation

Bill Log

________________ Month

✓	Date Paid	Bill Name	Amount	Due Date	Confirmation

Bill Log

_____________ Month

✓	Date Paid	Bill Name	Amount	Due Date	Confirmation

Bill Log

_______________ Month

✓	Date Paid	Bill Name	Amount	Due Date	Confirmation

Bill Log

_______________ Month

✓	Date Paid	Bill Name	Amount	Due Date	Confirmation

Bill Log

_______________ Month

✓	Date Paid	Bill Name	Amount	Due Date	Confirmation

Bill Log

________________ Month

✓	Date Paid	Bill Name	Amount	Due Date	Confirmation

Bill Log

_______________ Month

✓	Date Paid	Bill Name	Amount	Due Date	Confirmation

Bill Log

_______________ Month

✓	Date Paid	Bill Name	Amount	Due Date	Confirmation

Bill Log

__________________ Month

✓	Date Paid	Bill Name	Amount	Due Date	Confirmation

Bill Log

_________________ Month

✓	Date Paid	Bill Name	Amount	Due Date	Confirmation

Bill Log

_______________ Month

✓	Date Paid	Bill Name	Amount	Due Date	Confirmation

Bill Log

_______________ Month

✓	Date Paid	Bill Name	Amount	Due Date	Confirmation

Bill Log

_______________ Month

✓	Date Paid	Bill Name	Amount	Due Date	Confirmation

Bill Log

_________________ Month

✓	Date Paid	Bill Name	Amount	Due Date	Confirmation

Bill Log

______________ Month

✓	Date Paid	Bill Name	Amount	Due Date	Confirmation

Bill Log

_______________ Month

✓	Date Paid	Bill Name	Amount	Due Date	Confirmation

Bill Log

_________________ Month

✓	Date Paid	Bill Name	Amount	Due Date	Confirmation

Bill Log

___________________ Month

✓	Date Paid	Bill Name	Amount	Due Date	Confirmation

Bill Log

_______________ Month

✓	Date Paid	Bill Name	Amount	Due Date	Confirmation

Bill Log

_______________ Month

✓	Date Paid	Bill Name	Amount	Due Date	Confirmation

Bill Log

_________________ Month

✓	Date Paid	Bill Name	Amount	Due Date	Confirmation

Bill Log

_______________ Month

✓	Date Paid	Bill Name	Amount	Due Date	Confirmation

Bill Log

______________ Month

✓	Date Paid	Bill Name	Amount	Due Date	Confirmation

Bill Log

_______________ Month

✓	Date Paid	Bill Name	Amount	Due Date	Confirmation

Bill Log

_______________ Month

✓	Date Paid	Bill Name	Amount	Due Date	Confirmation

Bill Log

_______________ Month

✓	Date Paid	Bill Name	Amount	Due Date	Confirmation

Bill Log

_________________ Month

✓	Date Paid	Bill Name	Amount	Due Date	Confirmation

Bill Log

___________________ Month

✓	Date Paid	Bill Name	Amount	Due Date	Confirmation

Bill Log

_______________ Month

✓	Date Paid	Bill Name	Amount	Due Date	Confirmation

Bill Log

_______________ Month

✓	Date Paid	Bill Name	Amount	Due Date	Confirmation

Bill Log

________________ Month

✓	Date Paid	Bill Name	Amount	Due Date	Confirmation

Bill Log

________________ Month

✓	Date Paid	Bill Name	Amount	Due Date	Confirmation

Bill Log

_______________ Month

✓	Date Paid	Bill Name	Amount	Due Date	Confirmation

Bill Log

_______________ Month

✓	Date Paid	Bill Name	Amount	Due Date	Confirmation

Bill Log

_______________ Month

✓	Date Paid	Bill Name	Amount	Due Date	Confirmation

Bill Log

_______________ Month

✓	Date Paid	Bill Name	Amount	Due Date	Confirmation

Bill Log

_______________ Month

✓	Date Paid	Bill Name	Amount	Due Date	Confirmation

Bill Log

_______________ Month

✓	Date Paid	Bill Name	Amount	Due Date	Confirmation

Bill Log

_______________ Month

✓	Date Paid	Bill Name	Amount	Due Date	Confirmation

Bill Log

_______________ Month

✓	Date Paid	Bill Name	Amount	Due Date	Confirmation

Bill Log

_______________ Month

✓	Date Paid	Bill Name	Amount	Due Date	Confirmation

Bill Log

_______________ Month

✓	Date Paid	Bill Name	Amount	Due Date	Confirmation

Bill Log

_______________ Month

✓	Date Paid	Bill Name	Amount	Due Date	Confirmation

Bill Log

_________________ Month

✓	Date Paid	Bill Name	Amount	Due Date	Confirmation

Bill Log

______________ Month

✓	Date Paid	Bill Name	Amount	Due Date	Confirmation

Bill Log

______________ Month

✓	Date Paid	Bill Name	Amount	Due Date	Confirmation

Bill Log

_______________ Month

✓	Date Paid	Bill Name	Amount	Due Date	Confirmation

Bill Log

_______________ Month

✓	Date Paid	Bill Name	Amount	Due Date	Confirmation

Bill Log

__________________ Month

✓	Date Paid	Bill Name	Amount	Due Date	Confirmation

Bill Log

_______________ Month

✓	Date Paid	Bill Name	Amount	Due Date	Confirmation

Bill Log

______________ Month

✓	Date Paid	Bill Name	Amount	Due Date	Confirmation

Bill Log

_______________ Month

✓	Date Paid	Bill Name	Amount	Due Date	Confirmation

Bill Log

_______________ Month

✓	Date Paid	Bill Name	Amount	Due Date	Confirmation